Crystal Lighthouse Productions LLC
www.crystal-lighthouse.com

ISBN 978-0615910574

Cover art by Dr. Renuka Parmar
Cover and interior design by Devyani Seth

Printed by CreateSpace, an Amazon.com company

BEING
AUM

A collection of poems by
MINOTI ROY

Translated by
Mukteshwar Kshirsagar

CRYSTAL
LIGHTHOUSE
PRODUCTIONS

CONTENTS

PREFACE

The artisan bowed down and touched her feet not knowing why he was summoned. With a smile on her face, the Queen opened her treasure trove brimming with jewels. "You are the chosen one, pick what you can. Use your art and make me a necklace!" said she.

Similar was my fortune when one sunny morning, Minoti Roy, alias "Monima", asked me to do the translations of her Bengali poems, fully aware that I did not know the language. Then followed three memorable months of my life. She would explain a couple of poems at a time, word by word and as the meaning sank in, I would translate them in English. Understanding the Bengali text, trying to feel the emotions expressed and then casting them in a poetic form in English required hours of being in her energy field. Often, while getting into the narrative, I could see Monima getting into uplifting moods and reliving memories that would transport me to different worlds. I could feel a purifying effect taking place within me. I have attempted to express my gratitude in the following lines:

> Dear Monima,
> These couple of months I was on a voyage
> A voyage of joy
> A journey of revelation
> An excursion into realms unknown
> A passage into the play of myriad emotions!
>
> I witnessed the birth of a New Earth
> I danced with the gopis, full of mirth
>
> My chest swelled with pride of Indian glory
> I shuddered at the blaze of Kali's fury
>
> Shiva's Tandav, Shriram's temple bells
> Krishna's flute casting magical spells
>
> Ramkrishna Paramhansa's and Thakur Ravi's sight
> brightened up my world, with my eyes shut tight

I felt blessed to observe the cosmic union
Tears of gratitude blurring my vision

I have tried to capture the magic created by you
Please grace this work, my humble tribute to you

Thank you very much for assigning me this task
What more can anyone ask?

When the translation work was over, I sought her permission to compile the poems as a book. Monima agreed. Like the artisan, I selected 42 poems. As my understanding deepened, I discovered that, based on the common dominant sentiment, the poems could be grouped into five sections, which also aided convenience of presentation in the book. The sections are called—"At the feet of Masters", "The Musings", "The Call", "In Communion with Divinity" and "The Experience".

The last six poems in the section titled "The Experience" are like a crescendo in a symphony, a fitting climax to a body of heavenly music. Whereas in the case of commoners, many life cycles may pass without getting even a fleeting glimpse of the Divine, Monima recounts how on multiple occasions she is swept off her normal consciousness and visited by imagery of Divinity. "Spectacle of rising Kundalini", "The Yogic Vista" and "Worshipping the cosmic union" is the trilogy of poems capturing her three such out-of-the world experiences. Here she records all that unfolds in front of her and its impact on her Being.

Energy crystallizes to take a form displaying itself as matter and matter evolves transcending the form to become one with energy. Incarnation of the Supreme as a human being and the spiritual evolution of a human, culminating in dissolution into the Supreme are designs of Destiny. The final three poems, "In Sync with Shiva", "Playing with Ma Kali" and "With You in my Being—I become AUM", reverberate with the above thought leaving a discerning reader spellbound.

What could be an appropriate title for such a compilation? On display were various topics, a wide range of emotions and issues related to different sections of society such as men, women and youth. A title needs to reflect that which is common to all the creations in the book.

It transpired that the one thing common to all the poems is the State of Being of Monima. These poems have not been composed intellectually but they have *happened* to her after she had experienced the Divine. In the prologue "I am AUM" Monima says:

> However miniscule and worthless I may be
> I know deep within, I am part of thee

In "Worshipping the cosmic union" she records:

> My being expands to take in the world
> And then becomes the center stage

In "With You in my being—I become AUM" Monima closes by realizing:

> AUM was the beginning and beyond the end is AUM
> With You in my being I become AUM

In reverence to the fact that this entire literary creation has emanated from somewhere within her while she remained in an evolved state of existence, this collection of poems has been given the title "Being AUM".

I am thankful to my friends Krishna Solegaonkar, Snehal Solegaonkar, Kishore Kelekar, Trupti Kelekar and Vijay Parmar for their valuable suggestions after going through the manuscript. Heartfelt thanks are due to Devika Thakkar of Crystal Lighthouse Productions, USA, and Devyani Seth without whose enthusiastic encouragement and consummate technology and design support the publication of this book would not have been possible.

Adorning the cover is an oil-on-canvas painting by artist Dr. Renuka Parmar. It depicts the turmoil and churning of the Bhavasagar, i.e., ocean of life. From the churning rises the orb of knowledge, the Eternal AUM.

— **Mukteshwar Kshirsagar**

Mukteshwar Kshirsagar, former Deputy Director with the Times of India Group, is a disciple of Smt. Minoti Roy. An alumnus of I.I.T. Mumbai, he is a technocrat by training and has worked as a corporate executive with a career spanning 33 years. He expresses his worldview of human affairs in short stories, essays and poems in English, Hindi and Marathi.

FOREWORD

It is my honour to write this foreword to the book of poems by
Smt. Minoti Roy—Monima, as she is fondly called by those of us
whose lives she has touched. I had the good fortune of meeting her
more than a decade ago in February 2003. She is truly an embodiment
of unconditional motherly love for all. Her concern towards everyone
is remarkable. While being compassionate, I have seen her deal with
sternness when the situation demands. It is a sternness borne out of sheer
love. Like a sculptor, chiseling an idol out of stone, she works her magic
patiently on her ardent followers, carving out the divinity hidden in them,
with hard strokes where necessary.

Bengal, India has produced many jewels such as Thakurji
Ramkrishna Paramhansa and Rabindranath Tagore. These great souls
had a deep influence on and touched the lives of many, including Monima.
She was born and brought up in an atmosphere fully soaked in the love of
Thakurji. Her family had a close association with Thakurji and his wife,
Sharda Ma. Her inherent intensity, coupled with these *samskars*, resulted
in her experiencing divinity at a very tender age.

The *sahaj bhav* and *sakhya bhav* evident in her poems (such as in "O
Mother of mine", "Playing with Ma Kali", "Janmashtami") can be traced
to this introduction to the Divine in early childhood. Monima is at ease
worshipping the many images of God with total devotion. She converses
and invokes Krishna, Shiva, Durga, and even seemingly ferocious forms
such as Rudra or Kali with equal fondness. This is just like an innocent
child who is completely at home with many relatives. While engaged in
worshipping various forms of Divinity, she also feels herself to be the
Omnipotent Principle behind them, thus giving a glimpse of the Adwait
Philosophy. She aspires to merge with this Principle and that is her only
thirst. Her prayers are not asking for petty things but are soulful as one
can see in "Let me experience Your Grace" where she says:

> You bestow on me all the worldly riches
> But I thirst for the feel of your kind touches

or in "Forgive me", where she urges that she is not afraid of punishment but withers at the thought of abandonment.

As her intensity was deepening, her very faith provided her all necessary guidance. Just as she worships many Gods with devotion, she has utmost reverence for many Gurus—Ramkrishna Paramhansa, Mahavatar Babaji, Adi Shankaracharya and Rabindranath Tagore to name some of them. Not only has she always considered them to be her Gurus, but they have also given her their blessings in the form of direct instructions and guidance for further sadhana. This guidance came to her through dreams and vision. The complex Yogic practices and Kriya yoga were revealed to her through this mode. Contemporary experts in the field were astonished to learn that she has mastered so much without the help of a Guru in person. The indirect transmission seems to have been as powerful and effective as the direct. The poems in section V, "The Experience", stand testimony to this. The exotic experiences have been very vividly described in "The Yogic Vista" and "Worshipping the cosmic union".

As detailed in those poems, she often used to be in trance-like states. She had a divine vision of merging with that Principle as described in "The Vision". Generally people equate themselves with their body-mind complex only and ignore the divinity residing in them. Monima, on the other hand, highlights this divinity in "With You in my being—I become AUM" where she says:

> Deluded people think it's me they see
> Blind they are towards You besides me

It is noteworthy that Monima is not disconnected from the practical world. She feels pained looking at the selfishness in the world. Her call to the youth, reprimand to the hypocrite and thundering threat to those who ill-treat women in "Are you listening?" and "Thunder of Kali" are all indicators of this. Her purity and absolute innocence can be seen in her portrait of a new world in "The Birth of a New Earth".

The understanding and support of her husband was essential for this extraordinary life journey to be possible. It is for this reason she holds him also as one of her Gurus. She expresses her endless gratitude to all the Gurus. In her poem "Guru Shakti" she assures that:

> His (Guru's) aura of love will always bestow
> strength, peace and liberation on you

thus giving comfort and confidence to other seekers. At the same time, in "Beyond the mind—God you will find", she reminds us that:

Such (desireless) mind is your Guru, helps you keep pure

These poems are born of spontaneity without any intellectual interference. They were originally written in Bengali at least 25 years ago. Now she feels the time is ripe for this poetry to reach far and wide. With this in mind, a translation of these poems in English was thought of.

May all those who read the book, get touched by the poetry and in turn by Divinity.

— **Gauri Kshirsagar**

Gauri Kshirsagar, former Head, Dept. of Mathematics, R. Ruia College, Mumbai, is a gold medalist in mathematics at graduate and postgraduate levels and a Sanskrit Visharad. After excelling as a banker for 13 years, she took up a career in teaching. An ardent advocate of holistic education, she has strong spiritual leanings. Her literary repertoire includes textbooks in Mathematics and Marathi translations of teachings of Indian mystics such as Dada Gawand and her spiritual Guru, Swami Harish Madhukar.

PROLOGUE

I am AUM

What am I if not the least?
It's You and You alone that exists

Here and there, everywhere
In my very being, now and forever

I am just a wisp of water vapour
You are the massive cloud cover

I am nothing but a quivering droplet
And You are the boundless rolling ocean

A speck of dust is what I am
You are the mountain kissing the sky

I am a grass blade quaking in the wind
You are the forest, mysterious and deep

But however miniscule and worthless I may be,
I know, deep within, I am part of thee!

I am AUM, I am AUM, I am AUM

ॐ

– মা সরস্বতী –

তুমি মা অম্বিকা, জগৎ পালিকা
বড় মা এসে তুমি, সাজিয়া বর্মলিকা

কভু মা দশভূজে, সিংহ বাহিনী,
কভু মা ত্রয়ূহরে ত্রিলোক পালিনী ॥

মাগো ত্রিলোচনা, নগেন্দ্র নন্দিনী,
কৃপা করো মাগো, দুর্গতি নাশিনী।

তুমি মা ভৈরবী, তুমি মা ভবানী
আমি যে তোরই মাগো, শৈলেন্দ্র নন্দিনী।

তুই বীণাপাণি, বিদ্যা দায়িনী,
কভু মা সরস্বতী, কভু নারায়ণী।

আনন্দ দায়িনী মাগো, নাম নারায়ণী,
বিদ্যাদায়িনী মাগো, রস দৃষ্টি কারিনী
পূজি মাগো তোর ভৈরব-মন্দিরে।
পূজিব শুধু তোরে সুরের ঝঙ্কারে,
তোর সুর সাগরে ডুবিয়ে দে মা,
সার্থক হোক মোর সাধনা।

I

AT THE FEET OF MASTERS

Guru Shakti—the Power of the Master

*Monima has rock-solid faith in the power of a Guru. A Guru not
only guides from a distance like a lighthouse but also takes direct
command of his disciple's life like the captain of a ship. Due to his
blessing, one is able to surmount all obstacles and be successful.
Monima herein makes a passionate appeal to harbour no doubts
and surrender to the Guru.*

This world is an ocean,
        its rumbling waves heaving a sigh
My body is a frail vessel
        for crossing the tides mountain high

Guru is the lighthouse, Guru the captain
        he will blow breeze in my sails
I will then get the might and strength
        to defeat marauding sharks and whales

With complete faith in the wisdom of the Guru,
        my ship will embark on the voyage
Putting all nagging doubts to rest,
        at Guru's feet I seek my solace

Power of the Guru-mandal alone
        is the sole source of energy in self
Surrender at his feet and then watch,
        how success will display itself

Even in the wildest dreams, you cannot fathom
        in what form the Guru will reach you
He will appear with love, speak with love
        and with compassion, will embrace you

His aura of love will always bestow
    strength, peace and liberation on you
Why harbour any fears, my son,
    when His protection is the armour for you?

Thakur—the Kalpataru

*In an elevated mode of prayer, Monima showers accolades on
the Master out of deep reverence, and feels that the Master is the
proverbial Kalpataru, the mythical tree granting all desires of
those sitting beneath it.*

You returned from the mysterious unknown
      and at one glance recognized me
You were always there in that glow of light,
      but my tears rendered you unseen by me

Our land has seen a pantheon of sages
      you are an avatar after countless ages
Blissfully unaware of this though you are,
      I belong to you, O Mahavatar.

You are limitless, you are so great,
      yet you heard my small little plaint
When you ascend the trance-like state,
      you take upon yourself all our pain

You are the almighty,
      you are my fate
As proclaimed by Jogeshwari Bhairavi,
      you, Gurudev, are the Supreme Incarnate

Incarnation of the Divine Supreme

Thakur Ramkrishna Paramhansa is central to Monima's Guru-
mandal. Herein she pays homage to his role as a seer who
maintained that all religions lead to the same fundamental Truth.

Thou art the emperor of the universe
Revered and worshipped by the world
You grace me with all that is gold
Make my destiny and let it unfold

I bow to thee—Thakur my Guru

You are the lighthouse for my ship
Let any fierce storm brew
I have a rock-solid faith that
The formless Spirit resides in you

I bow to thee—Thakur my Guru

We behold in you, Incarnation of the Supreme,
As the great Jogeshwari Bhairavi proclaimed
Dissolver of discord and creator of harmony
That's your role, universally acclaimed

I bow to thee—Thakur my Guru

Gist of every religion,
All pardoning and ever so kind
Solace for the tormented and helpless
Members of the whole of mankind

I bow to thee—Thakur my Guru

In praise of Thakur

Monima harbours not an iota of doubt that Thankur Ramkrishna
Paramhansa was God reborn. Since the age of seven, when
Ramkrishna appeared in her dreams, she considers him her Guru.
Being in an exalted state of existence, she understands the Divine,
whereas mundane people around her indulge in ridicule, out of
sheer ignorance. Unfazed by these, Monima envisions both
Vishnu, the sustainer, and Shiva, the dissolver, in Thakur.

Born again on the earth as Thakur,
　　　God appeared in Kamarpukur anon
Ramkrishna Paramhansa was his name,
　　　a true-blue stoic the world has ever known

Honor or insult didn't make any dent
　　　as you were far above the sentimental ground
I know, but not the world around does
　　　that you are the essence of all that goes around

With immense love in your bosom you came
　　　and gave me relief from all my pain
Only because of you, my Thakur,
　　　the demon of my ego has seen its end

My heart bleeds when I hear
　　　people say you got high on grass
Ignorant fools just cannot fathom
　　　that yours was a state of celestial trance

You elevate and grant solace
　　　to all the humble who seek your grace
At times you're Lord Vishnu spinning his chakra
　　　and sometimes you become Shiva the great

Jai ho Thakur!

Vishwaguru Adi Shankaracharya

Monima offers her prayers to Adi Shankaracharya, the foremost
Hindu spiritual philosopher who revived and spread Adwait
philosophy (non-dualism) all over; he was considered to be an
incarnation of Lord Shiva.

Serene and still like the Pacific Ocean
Purer than the morning dew
Eternal like the Universal Soul
More handsome than eyes ever knew

That's you—O my Guru

Master of scriptures, exponent of the Vedas
Poignant and intense like a burning flame
Renouncing the earthly, rejecting the lure,
You crossed the seas to resounding acclaim

That's you—O my Guru

Proclaiming religion as a way of life
Showing the world a real Brahman
Propounding that all is one
Incarnation indeed of ultimate Atman

That's you—O my Guru

Your birth being the Divine Design,
We bow to your Highness time and again
Fortunate are your father and mother
Blessed is the human race yet again

Mahavatar Babaji

*The ageless Himalayan Master Mahavatar Babaji initiated
Monima into Kriya Yoga. Here she pays her tribute to him and
entreats him to enable her to realize her destiny.*

In the pitch-dark night
    You light up my path
Everything I know
    is all what You taught

While blessing me with bounty
    You keep testing me
Whenever slightest danger lurks
    You are the one to protect me

You are my Guru, Mahavatar Babaji

With every breath of mine
    Your fragrance I inhale
And purer I become
    every time I exhale

You move with my subtle being
    thousands of miles in space
And always bring me home
    again safely to my base

You emerge on the earth
    every time in a form anew
But at the core You remain the same
    an innocent child, pure as dew

Ravaging Time bows to you
      be it past, present or future to come
While others stay but a fleeting moment
      You alone are the permanent one

You are the Divine Author
      and the world acts out your writ
Can even a ripple arise
      lest that is your express wish?

You ordained for me
      a purpose so bright
Life cycles have lapsed
      but continues the fight
You know I have struggled
      with all my might
Yet the end, so elusive
      is nowhere in sight

Please grace me
      at least in this birth
And let me honour
      my purpose on earth

Jai ho my Guruji, Jai ho my Babaji!

Thakur Rabindranath

In a testimony to her ability to transcend the real-time world and get guidance from past masters, Monima here sets up contact with Rabindranath Tagore whom she has never met. While offering prayers to him, she also displays a firm belief that her prayers have the power to recall the master back into the world.

My ship is steered by Masters
      some without a form
You are like the Pole Star
      leading me through the storm

Gales and hurricanes may
      lash me with all their might
I survive this tough voyage
      solely due to your guiding light

Never have I seen you
      for real by my eyes
But your image is enshrined
      forever in my mind

I am a little nobody
      so feeble and frail
That you are my savior
      is my only strength

My language falls short
      to spell feelings of mine
You inspire me to try
      and pen down these lines

You dispel the darkness
    and brighten up my world
The rays of your wisdom
    shine on all I behold

You are the light
    and you are the source
Blessed is the world
    to beget such a soul

Transcending all barriers
    you are the Universal kind
Having left the mortal body
    you are alive in its mind

My faith tells me

God will ask you to return
    hearing you pray
Once you come back
    don't ever go away
Accept my endless gratitude
    and bless me all the way

Jai Gurudev!

Remembering Rabindranath on ascension day

*Rabindranath Tagore is a part of Monima's revered Guru-mandal.
In this lilting musical homage Monima remembers his ascension
to another dimension and acknowledges that she owes her very
being and everything around, to him.*

Every year on the 22nd day of Shravan
      as the sun paints the sky golden
I pray and go down memory lane
      reminiscing about those days olden

I am surrounded and get overwhelmed
      by all that's your reflection around
All this world is but your play,
      reverberating with light and sound

Meditating pulse of your mind-state
      touches and engulfs my very core
And that becomes the fountainhead
      for a soulful music of your lore

The words may be mine
      but language belongs to you
I surrender and dissolve myself fully
      to celebrate and enjoy merging with you

II

THE MUSINGS

The Birth of a New Earth

*Fragmentation along sectarian, religious or ideological lines has
made our world full of strife and misery. It is like darkness at noon.
Monima, who had a glimpse of Utopia in her meditative state,
calls upon people not to despair but fire their imagination to
conceive of a new order, with the hope that the power of collective
thought will help in making the vision a reality.*

Imagine ... the Birth of a New Earth

No conflicts, no contradictions
Only the good will remain
All will rise above themselves
And truth alone will prevail

Imagine ... the Birth of a New Earth

None will cheat, nor will stray
There will arise a new human race
No petty minds, no thoughts vile
Spiritual core sprouting pure New Life

Imagine ... the Birth of a New Earth

Destruction of discrimination, breaking down the walls
No pain anywhere, just love for all
One world, one race, one spirit, one soul
Pristine pure life will be the sole goal

Imagine ... the Birth of a New Earth

I dream of such a New Earth
When will it rise?
Touch of the Divine
When will it bring light?

Our world will be a heaven
With no angst and nothing foul
Body be mortal, but immortal soul
Will never perish and ever remain whole

Happiness, freedom, peace and mirth
Imagine ... the Birth of a New Earth

The Sextet of Enemies

Monima points out six ignoble impulses that can destroy
tranquility of the mind and calls them the sextet of enemies.
She cautions that rather than any external enemy, harm to
the Self may be caused by this sextet.

You get armed to the teeth
      to fight the invader's plunder
Unaware of the evil sextet within
      that is set to loot and thunder
Ignoring its threat
      will be the ultimate blunder
Who are these six
      do you ever wonder?

They are greed, anger, attachment, jealousy,
      lust and egoistic pride

Watch out for these six
      who will always hound you
Falling prey to them
      is sure to scald you
Golden glades have wilted
      and turned a desert dune
Legion are such lives
      damned to doom

Greed paves the way to an untimely end
      snuffing out debt-ridden and miserably living men

Anger drives many down the path of sin
      dumping sense and sanity in the wayside bin

Attachment will cause an emotional delusion
    unleashing a life-long chase of mirage and illusion

Jealousy will pollute minds that are pure
    Succumbing to its lure will be disastrous for sure

Fangs of lust will tear you in tatters,
    hence worship beauty within, not the external glitter

Egoistic pride will decimate all your wealth
    Steer away from it for your happiness and health

Falling prey to this sextet
    will unleash all pain
Be aware and control them
    for your own ultimate gain

I Love

*Common people, due to their limited awareness, can play out only
one role at a time on this stage called life. But Monima, with her
polyangular awareness, can be like a curious child at one moment
and appeal to the Universal Mother the next moment. This is borne
out amply in this poem where she goes looking for her favourite
things. Be it beautiful flowers, the chatter of children or an all-
encompassing feeling of love for humanity.*

Deep blue dome of the sky
Woolly clouds sailing by
Carpet of the grass, green and plane
Sparkling fresh with drops of rain

Blossoms of flowers in glowing tints
A kite swirling high, spreading its wings
Gobbledygook of kids on swings
Peals of their laughter and the joy it brings

Speaking truth always, with love as the spark
Walking the talk ever, no matter how harsh
Wishing well for all and meeting noble souls
This love for all is what makes me whole

What brings in my focus is pure love
What defines my locus is nothing but love
To light up the world with the power of love
Every moment I love all that I love

Are you listening?

*Many seem inclined to put up a facade of pious behavior than
be serious about real internal changes. Monima is amused and
suggests a correction.*

Responding to social norms,
        dressing up in a hermit's best
Taking on an image of a faithful
        saffron proclaiming your ascetic state

Outer whitewash is neatly done
        but how about purity of heart?
Conquest of the sensory lure alone
        will entitle you to the saffron mark

Beware, the mind is fleeting and vain
        you will do well to put it on rein
Before rushing for your neighbour's liberation
        Why not work on self-elevation?

Why is Kali Ma dark?

*Kali is the ferocious form of the Sacred Feminine who takes birth
to protect her children and kill the demons representing evil.
Monima vividly portrays her vision of Ma Kali. She warns the
seeker that individuals must live out their destiny and only then
will they be worthy of the grace of Kali.*

To grasp your true nature
       is certainly not child's play
You stepping on Lord Shiva,
       a potent image, what does it say?

Ties of the mundane world
       shackle and chain us to the ground
Pray come, release us all
       from the grip of the enemies around

Vanquished demons' skulls in the pond
       send shivers up our spine and chest
And there you stand, up in arms,
       garland of the skulls around your neck

We fall prey to our foes with fright
       and get assaulted left, center and right
The all-powerful Mother then takes birth
       and banishes the evil from face of the earth

She consumes the monsters causing menace,
       gobbles them up and frees the human race
Brilliance of the Mother dazzles the sight,
       not easy to look at, she is so bright

She kills the demons, drinks blood like a predator
       and then she unleashes a deafening laughter
That resonates in the universe with triumph of a victor

By killing the killer she protects us all
        filling our lives with celestial mirth
Complete surrender at her pious feet
        will resurrect the troubled from cycles of birth

Mother's mercy showers on all
        be he the highest or lowliest of all
She'll pick you up and take you on her lap
        will cajole you at times or let you sometimes fall
Everything she does is for benefit of all

Sometimes she loves, at times she plays
        sometimes she slaps, at times she slays
No one can know what lies in fate
        but Mother is always there watching one's state

Forefront is not for her, she stays behind
        you have to walk the path, you have to mind
At times your chosen way, may lead to hell
        it's then for you to seek pardon and tell.

Ma will then pick you up and wipe you clean
Love you and bring you back from the den of the Mean

She is the savior, she bears the brunt
        of all our sins and miserable stunts
She takes upon her all our venom stark
        is it then any wonder why She is so dark?

Beyond the mind—God we will find

Having a firsthand experience of forays into the realm of the
Divine, Monima reveals that silencing the chattering mind is
the only path leading to the truth. She also goes on to say that
such a quietened mind permits prompting of higher energy
and becomes your inner Guru.

Ages have lapsed but few could find
A sure shot key to tackle the mind

He who can curb the mind's excesses
Does not crave for material success

The treacherous mind plots a trip of the senses
Hence conquest of the mind is truly the essence

Control the chatter and quieten the mind
Worldly lures can't then put you in a bind

Watch how the wolves of greed recede away
Desires will no more, then, have their sway

A lamp glows steady when the wind doesn't blow
So stills the mind when desires don't flow

Such mind is your Guru, helps you keep pure
Quiet mind and clear conscience will elevate you for sure

From elements you arise, in elements you dissolve
Experiencing Divinity in every form, make it your firm resolve

The Master stroke

Complete surrender to a Guru becomes very tough because of the play of one's ego. Monima indicates here that a disciple only needs to overcome this hurdle and then the rest becomes the responsibility of the Guru.

Surrender at the Master's feet
     thoughts, emotions, your entire being
Unmindful of the Master waiting for you,
     hey ignoramus, where are you going?

Reeling under the burden of ego
     your tired self yearns for relief
But you are unaware that the kind master
     is right there, for those who believe

He is there, waiting for his children
     to mend their ways and come home to him
All you need is to carry on working
     and joyously leave the rest to him

You just have to do your duty
     and soulfully ask to be forgiven by him
Pray to the Lord, surrender to the master
     and soak in the blessings showered by him

Lessons of Astral Travel

Realized persons, on the journey of liberation, are endowed
with yogic powers. The ability of astral travel is one such power.
Monima gives the reader a glimpse into her experiences of
astral travel.

Flying with the wings of the wind
          my astral self travels far apace
Crossing rivers and mountains on earth
          I traverse the ethereal vacuum in space

I streak across the deep blue sky
          studded with twinkling stars
Hearing as they call me out
          beckoning me with outstretched arms

I can cover a million miles
          but not a soul can spot me
I can respond to anybody's call
          but no one can hear me

One who is fully in sync with Him
          can surely catch a glimpse of mine
He who lives in alert awareness
          will never ever miss the sign

This wandering of mine has opened my eyes
          that not many recall my name with love
I am blamed for their misery
          and barbs of abuse are hurled above

Thank you my Lord for enabling my voyage
that brought home the reality to me
Blissfully ignorant I would have remained
of the folly of doctrine adopted by me.

শোন শোন তরুণদয়, ধ্যানের সন্তানগন,
     তোমাদের কাছে রাখি মোর ছোট্ট নিবেদন।
খন্ড খন্ড ভারত হোক একত্র আবার,
     সবার কাছে এই প্রার্থনা জানাই বারবার।
ছেড় ছেড় গৃহী মোরা, ছেড় মোদের বাসনা
     তাই দিয়ে পূর্ণ হবে বন্ধু মোদের ধারনা।
সনাতন এক ধ্যান নিকেতন দেখি বারংবার,
     ইচ্ছা র'ল করার তাই প্রতিষ্ঠা তাহার।
সর্ব ধর্মের অনেক গিরি করবে আশ্রয় বসে ধ্যান,
     কেন গৌরবময় থাকবে নাকো সবার সমান স্থান।
নানান গুরুর ছবি বিক্রি করবে না কেউ উপার্জনে,
     মাটি'গুলো নিয়ে কেউ করবে নাকো হানাহানি।
সবার ইষ্ট তার আছে নিজের অন্তরেই,
     সবাই এক হবে তারা একটু ধ্যানে বসলেই।
ধ্যানে ধ্যানে গড়ে উঠুক ধ্যান নিকেতন
     সব মানুষই হয়ে উঠুক এক এক ভগবান।

III

THE CALL

Call for Youth

*Realizing that so-called "tradition" is a burden that inhibits
progress, Monima displays a forward-looking temper by calling
upon youth to summon courage to destroy the archaic and
ring in a fresh dawn of awakening.*

Get up ye youth and shed your stupor
Don't you see tears in the eyes of your mother?

Stir up and energize your hidden power
Respond to the call of the Universal Seer

Unleash the typhoon and take up the charge
Let the aged rest and ahead you march

Dynamite the old and construct the new
Use your muscle to make dreams come true

You lack nothing, just peek within self
Dump the begging bowl and feel your strength

Discover, unshackle and realize your spunk
Why act like a blind man who is also drunk?

Don't wallow in the sorrow
Brought on by your sloth, my boy

Shake off the slumber
Spread your wings
and fly into the radiant sky

You are the youthful men and women
Boundless energy is your true domain

Dormant volcano simmers in your gut
Blast away the yokel and let the fire erupt

If you wake up, all will join
What will then cloud the bright sunshine?

Demolish the demons of hesitation and fear
Banish the ego from far and near
Life at the highest level is solely yours
Prove worthy of His Grace, by realizing your power

Anguish of a suffering soul

Mindless selfishness and petty pursuits of ignorant multitudes
cause immense agony to Monima, especially since Truth has
dawned upon her early. Her elevated state of consciousness,
while providing a ray of hope, also cements her belief that she
is not meant for the mundane world.

Hey my omnipotent Lord,
          the spirit shining bright
I live in a dark tunnel
          without a chink of light

Why grant me a human life
          that is nothing but a tragedy?
Isn't it a paradox of sorts
          or a plain, simple parody?

Wherever I cast my eyes
          I spot only a dance of greed
Selfishness is so rampant
          any religion, any creed

All are busy in hot pursuit
          of self-serving madness
Mine is a loner's lament
          getting lost in wilderness

O Destiny, please reveal to me
          why do I thus suffer?
In this world of falsehood
          a misfit like me has nothing to offer

❧

Let me experience Your Grace

Engaged in a deep communion with Divinity, Monima seeks help for annihilation of the ego as the only boon. Setting aside worldly wealth, she pines for experience of His Grace alone as the sole objective of her quest through repeated cycles of birth.

You decimate the monster of my ego
          make me, my false pride, forgo
I have eyes only for you, my Lord
          let me experience Your Grace, O God

Every journey ends
          at your beautiful, nimble feet
Since eons I am in search
          of their divine seat

You bestow on me all the worldly riches
          but I thirst for the feel of your kind touches
I may be the only one cherishing this wish
          your blessing alone will give me everlasting peace

I'll bear any pain
          to keep on singing your praise
To catch your fragrance
          even if it's a trace
O Lord of mine
          let me just once experience Your grace

Thunder of Kali

*After witnessing an episode of male hooligans causing
immense trouble to a young girl, Monima transcends the
state of helplessness and becomes thundering Kali, the all-
vanquishing Goddess. She delivers this powerful reprimand
to the tyrannical males of the world.*

I talk for the women of this globe
The real power that runs all homes
You fail to see my glimpse in her flesh
As you think I exist in idols of stones?

How will you ever know my reality?
All the five elements make me mighty
Even Shiva once failed to see this truth
You are just a mortal, doomed to death

You have succumbed to all inner foes
What worth is your worship then, if not full of woes?

Worse than animals is your conduct, you fool,
            discrediting your parents' name
A blot on humanity is what you are
            putting whole mankind to shame

With a sweeping stroke of my sword
            I will behead you, tyrant male
And then by just my bare hands
            lap up your blood ending your trail

Arise O Rudra

Lord Shiva is envisioned as a recluse known for his world-renouncing ways. Monima here is in communion with him, entreating him to grant his grace to mankind.

Awaken and arise O Kailaspati Shiva
Do not stay stuck in dhyana and yoga

You are the constant, You are the complete
Pray reach down to us, O Maheshwar

Flood our dark world with the light of Truth
How long will you be silent and mute?

Hidden you are by covers all round
What will happen if you are not found?

Please come, come running
O my savior Rudra
I am afire, I am burning
save me O my Hara

Prayer to the Lord

*In an evolved state of awareness, Monima sees the Lord as pure
love, convinced that she is completely one with him. She is full of
love towards every part of the Existence around. Her only prayer to
the Lord is to allow this love to stay within her core forever.*

A ripple of love, a wave of love
　　　　an ocean of love, that's what you are
The world we view, the universe beyond
　　　　seen in every form, that's who you are

Encompassing the body I dote,
　　　　filling up my mind that floats
Deeply seated in the space of my conscience,
　　　　occupying my Being, that is where you are

In every droplet of water on earth,
　　　　in every inch of the ground on earth,
In every piece of the blue firmament,
　　　　You are the soul and You are the content

Be it the light, be it the shadow,
　　　　the air I breathe or the toxin I throw,
The depth of my mind, or the core of my life,
　　　　You are in every atom—that is my firm belief

God almighty, showering mercy on me
　　　　my only prayer, please thou grant
That never ever you will cast me away
　　　　and forever stay within my heart

IV

IN COMMUNION
WITH DIVINITY

Ode to the Supreme

*Monima expresses her world-view of the primordial energy that
runs the Universe. This energy shapes our destiny; some may call
it Shiva-Shakti while others may equate it with the Divine trinity
of Brahma, Vishnu and Mahesh.*

This universe is your dynamic creation,
        ever convulsing in throes of transformation
Cyclically you arrive to lead the charge,
        every time in a different garb

You are the Purush, the revered Masculine
        but oft come disguised as the Sacred Feminine
Creator, sustainer and dissolver of all,
        you are the reason, you are the cause

Though you don't have a form of your own,
        You are there in every bit of our state
You are the boatman saving us from flood
        Skipper of our destiny and Captain of our fate

O Mother of mine

Monima sends out a call to Shakti, the Sacred Feminine, not to abandon her. She is convinced that grace of the Goddess is her right by birth.

Where have you gone,
    O Mother of mine
Leaving your child alone
    in this cruel world of thine?

O Mother of mine,
    I am not a beggar
Can the princess of a queen
    ever be a pauper?

I know I am Tara,
    O Mother of mine
But without you I am nil,
    let me glow in your shine

Pick me up in your lap,
    O Mother of mine
Who will wipe my tears
    and then make me smile?

Please come running,
    O Mother of mine
Come here
    Ma Bhavani, O Mother of mine

At the feet of the Mother

In one of Monima's poignant portrayals of her own state of being
when in a meditative mood, she offers obeisance to the Goddess
and expresses heartfelt gratitude for the divine gift of life.

The sacred pair of your crimson feet
        watching with teary eyes, O what a treat!

As a deity installed in my lotus-heart,
        I keep her awash in my tear-bath

The nectar of your remembrance, O Mother,
        drips into me throughout the day
Meditating on your beautiful feet
        keeps all mindless thoughts at bay

A dazzling flash of your resplendent face
        makes my eyes go on an insane spin
And when I offer the blue lotus bloom
        my eyes focus on your lovely feet twin

Every moment of my living state,
        with my every single heart beat
Full of gratitude for your gift of life
        I remember your pious feet

An offering

Acknowledging that every bit of the external world is nothing but a creation of the Divine, Monima engages fully in its search within herself. What she longs for is complete dissolution of her self into the Universal Principle.

I long for your glimpses
      in the lyrics that I find
As I stay engaged in your prayer
      within the sanctuary of my mind

You are ever present there
      in all matter at every state
Yet searching for you within me
      remains my perennial quest

Mother, Father and Brother of mine
      be with me forever
Can I forget you even for a moment?
      Never, till life is no more

You are visible in all I survey
      and not limited to an image
How can an idol contain you
      when the whole world is your stage?

I am not alone and all are mine
      Let me live this glorious trust
Devoid of violence, bereft of jealousy,
      make my world peaceful and just

Let me lose myself in you,
      what I reflect is your glory
That You compose the Universal mind
      is the beginning and end of every story

The eternal quest

Monima, having realized the true purpose of life at an early age,
goes in search of Divinity. She yearns for glimpses of Gurus such as
Ramkrishna Paramhansa or Gods such as Shiva, Kali and Krishna,
fully aware that all different forms represent one common energy.
She understands that what is manifest is not of any permanence.

O Brahman, when you take a human form,
    it's all your Leela—the Divine Play
Grant me the favor of getting your glimpse
    and release me from this worldly stay

You arrive as Ramkrishna Thakur
    You are Gadadhar, the life force in me
Now you are Kali, at times my Shiva
    Pulsating energy all around me

Under the canopy of a peepal tree
    Sits a cowherd talking to his mates
I know it is You and nobody but You
    O Madhusudan, reveal thy state

Your speech is dripping nectar
    your sound is so very sweet
How much I look for you high and low
    sobbing and crying, roaming the street

Since the first breath I drew on earth
    My quest is on with deep sangfroid
And whenever I think I found you, Krishna
    You vanish into the boundless void

Will it be then an Eternal Quest?
What is the answer, you know it best

Forgive me

*Monima pleads for forgiveness from the Lord by declaring that
she does not mind any punishment for inadvertent wrongdoing
but withers at the idea of being abandoned.*

Forgive me, my Lord
      have mercy on this ardent devotee
If I ever tread a wrong path
      let your wrath fall on me

Do punish me, my Lord
      but please don't abandon me
For if you desert me
      this world will turn a desert for me

Without your presence in my life
      even seven heavens will be void for me
Life after life I beseech, my Lord
      let my abode be at your sacred feet

Forgive me my Lord, please forgive me

Gopal

In a heightened and all-pervading sentiment of Love, Monima dons various roles, while revering the Universal Principle in different forms. Here she perceives it as Lord Shrikrishna or Gopal and offers her prayers becoming one with Yashoda, the foster mother, Radha, the consort, or Meera, the legendary devotee of the Lord.

When I am awake I see Gopal
In my dreams I meet Gopal
Apple of my eye, that is Gopal

Gopal is the light, bright as the noon
Gopal is darkness wrapping up the moon
Gopal is here, Gopal is there
Pulsating energy, Gopal is everywhere

Worship Gopal, remember Gopal
Gopal alone is the essence of parts
In absence of Gopal, without Gopal
The whole universe will break apart

Jai Gopal!

Janmashtami

*Raas Krida is the enchanting dance performed by Krishna
surrounded by gopis, his childhood playmates. Responding
to their ardent fervor of love and devotion, Krishna multiplies
himself and simultaneously dances with every gopi, submerging
the devout gopis in celestial ecstasy. Engulfed by a similar fervor
of devotion, Monima herein asks the Lord, "Will you come and
dance with me?"*

O my God, the Lord of my life,
     will you come and dance with me?

You may come with masculine pace
     Or you may wear feminine grace
I will take up any color for me,
     will you come and dance with me?

My being will waltz in sync with you,
     swaying to the magical music spun by you
Rhythm of drums will be haunting me
     will you come and dance with me?

Replete with affection, you anchor love
     this Universal emotion unites all in one
I feel your presence every moment near me,
     will you come and dance with me?

You will let me rest at your feet—no doubt
     Floating in my own tears, here I seek you out
I know for sure, you care for me,
     will you now come and dance with me?

❧

Yogeshwar Guru

*Monima sings the praise of Lord Shrikrishna in the form of the
supreme Yogi. On the one hand, she knows that the Omniscient is
her very own; at the same time, she prays and pleads with him not
to disown her. This is yet another instance of the ease with which
the blithe spirit of devotion enables Monima to move from being
the Seeker to being the one sought after.*

Yogeshwar Krishna, playing the flute
          you cast your spell on the world around
You cause every heart to beat and
          protect everything from sky to ground

Whatever that happens moment to moment
          is nothing but your own will
You exist in every single atom
          whether in motion or just standing still

You are the father, you are the mother,
          you are the brother, you are my very own
Here I completely surrender at your feet, Krishna,
          please accept my offering and do not disown

The world is but your creation
          and you are the Savior of all
Who else will rush to the rescue of the fallen?
          None but you, Divine Father of all

Whatever that is, is nothing else
          but a precious gift from you
So pristine is the nature around
          because it is just a reflection of you

When it emanates from the depths of the heart,
        you respond to every call
While living out the turmoil of life
        at your crimson feet we fall

Jai Yogeshwar!

V

THE EXPERIENCE

He—God of the Universe

*Monima paints a powerful picture of what she understands to
be the attributes of the Ultimate Energy called God. While letting
out the simple secret that can lead to His discovery, Monima also
reveals her glorious non-duality within.*

Who is He?

He comes from nowhere and exists everywhere
Yet few can feel his presence anywhere
He is seen in every form
Present is He in all the forms
Universe is His playground
In every bit only He is found

Who is He?

Fire of desire
Will destroy peace of your mind
Desirelessness is the only way
Soon you will find

Duality is an illusion,
all are but one
Enjoy, everything belongs to you,
Different is none

In this act of His
you are just a speck of scum
Much fragmented though you are
your Awareness is a continuum

Live out the human life
As destiny calls out for
Have faith in the formless He,
then salvation is not far

Who is He?

He is nothing but me

You are the Infinite

Swachchandanath *is a synonym of Lord Shiva. It highlights that
everything manifest or unmanifest in this universe is governed by
His will. Monima displays complete understanding of this Infinity,
which is the only thing of permanence, everything else being
transient. Monima's comprehension has evolved out of a direct
experience of the unknown.*

You are the Infinite *Swachchandanath*
       granting seekers' wish a thousand fold
I am just a limited Being,
       give me only that which I can hold

If you shower on me
       more than my fill,
How do I sustain?
       Pray guide me at your will

You grant me the kingdom's riches
       My abject poverty leaving no trace
Though bedecked in your divine jewels
       I yearn for the alms of your grace

Everything I do, whenever I do,
       I do it for you, I pray to you
Whenever I touch you in meditative state
       all my pain is quelled by you

I suffer cycles of death and birth,
       exit and enter as per your wish
Permanent thou are, there on the center stage
       all of us only players in transit

Thousands of years have gone
      and thousands more yet to pass
You are the Constant Infinite One
      my direct experience does the talk

The Vision

This is a very rare example of a first person account of a divine
experience that happened to Monima when she was alone in
a room at Asansole on one afternoon of 1973.

I opened my eyes and saw you there
      standing tall on my right
The room was glowing in luminous splendor
      like thousand suns shining bright

You were the source of the brilliance
      that had flooded my humble home
A fragrance from the Garden of Heaven
      was swirling up to the overhead dome

I was awestruck and became speechless
      Was it for real or just another dream?
With eyes wide open as if in trance
      my tears started pouring in a stream

Whom can I tell what happened to me,
      to whom can I explain the pleasurable pain?
I remained stunned and grateful forever
      my vision of THAT ... my eternal gain

Worshipping the cosmic union

Monima's outpouring after the opening of the Third Eye vision. She witnesses the ultimate union of Shiva and Shakti, which happens at her supreme center called Sahasrar.

Turning inwards my extroverted senses
        opens up my third eye vision
Then I become a privileged witness
        of Shiva and Shakti's cosmic union

I perform this worship
        at the altar of my mind
Blessings of the Guru
        steer my steps
Till the divine temple I find

My Being expands to take in the world
        and then becomes the center-stage
Heaven, earth and elements together
        orchestrate a divine symphony on stage

From the depth rises a coiled serpent,
        luminous white with silver scales
A brilliant diamond atop its head,
        strewn scales forming a lotus-bed

This pulsating energy rises through me
        piercing seven chakras with a mission
The final merger of Kundalini with Kameshwar
        happens at Sahasrar with ecstatic explosion

Spectacle of rising Kundalini

This is a graphic narration of what Monima undergoes upon rising of the Kundalini Shakti. For better comprehension of the poem, understanding of some symbology enshrined in Hindu Yoga shastra may be useful.

- *Human beings are the only species capable of transcending to higher levels of consciousness by meditation.*
- *Along the spinal cord are located seven centers of energy, called chakras. They are normally dormant. The five lower centers correspond to the five elements, i.e., Earth, Water, Fire, Air and Space. The sixth chakra is in the location of the Third Eye (i.e., between the eyebrows) and is called Agya Chakra. The seventh chakra is called Sahasrar (i.e., of thousand petals). It is located at the crown of the head. It is considered as the Supreme center of contact with God.*
- *Kundalini is the Corporeal energy lying coiled at the base of the spine. It is envisioned as a Goddess and has the form of a sleeping silver serpent.*
- *The arousal of Kundalini is indicative of advent on a spiritual path. It is implied that when this energy gets active, it rises up the spinal cord, activating the seven chakras one by one. The chakras open up with the passage of this energy. The meeting of Kundalini with Shiva happens at the seventh chakra and leads to ultimate enlightenment.*
- *The swan is a symbol of ultimate knowledge.*
- *The lotus symbolizes the spirit of ever-retaining purity unaffected by surrounding negativity.*
- *The sensory perception of two eyes enables viewing of normal objects. For extra sensory perception of higher visions, the Third Eye needs to be opened. The opening of the Third Eye vision is possible only by grace of a Guru.*

Holy Mother appeared today
     in the form of a graceful snake
A luminous, shining white one,
     her body covered with silver scales

Ensconced on her regal hood,
     a magnificent shining diamond large
Radiating glow of such splendor
     lighting up the space at large

My tears of gratitude,
     like a river they flow
Silver scales shed by you
     form a white lotus afloat

You carry the nectar of life,
     which sets off the ascent
You rise and keep rising,
     leaving behind sandalwood scent

No flowers nor leaves
     I need for your worship
Body, mind, my whole being
     is laid down at your feet

Arise, Ma Kundalini,
     On me let your blessings shower
Release me from my bondage of ages
     and awaken my hidden power

Energize my dormant centers,
     kindly dispel all the gloom
Let the sun of knowledge rise,
     let the world brighten and bloom

May your aura shine bright
     and make me glow from my core
Let the twin wings of knowledge and devotion
     carry me through heaven's door

The Yogic Vista

Monima portrays the visions that lay out in front of her after the Kundalini is awakened. She pleads to her Guru to open her Third Eye so that she can revel in the vista.

Wave upon wave is rolling in,
    cascading around the breathless me
I strive hard to keep afloat,
    but the surging waves submerge me

In a flash of a moment I see
    an enormous flame dazzling bright
And cruising on the waves of light
    is a majestic swan brilliantly white

Royally blooming in all its beauty,
    a white lotus with flowering petals
And wrapped around the swan and lotus,
    a serpent slithering like molten metal

Hey Gurudev, have mercy on me
    and pray open my third eye intense
I will then turn it inwards and revel
    in this vision to my heart's content

In Sync With Shiva

*In an exalted state, Monima recognizes that Shiva, the principle,
is omnipresent and also experiences that her own being contains
the Universal expanse, a paradigm of absolute synchronicity.*

Beyond comprehension you are,
        O Umapati Maheshwar
You make the universe dance
        to your tune, O Nateshwar

Be it a droplet of water,
        be it any obscure place
It's you and you alone
        that make up the entire space

You are present here and yonder
        that alone is the ultimate truth
Much before the beginning and long after the end
        only you exist, it's a fact and not a myth

You are rooted in my Sahasrar,
        in a resplendent, beautiful form of thee
And rest of me is traversed by
        Your life-breath circling in and around me

Center to me in the navel I find
        You again in a chakra form,
while you are striding all galaxies
        the raised trident in your arm

Sometimes you are ablaze with blinding fury
    playing the role of angry Rudra
Otherwise you are serene and peaceful,
    an all-pervading Shiva Shankar

I bow down to you, O my Lord!

Playing with Ma Kali

Having realized the elusive nature of the Universal energy in the form of playful Ma Kali, Monima comes up with a brilliant plan to embed Kali within her being. She is sure that her devotion will finally win.

Wearing saffron like ascetics and seers,
        adorning your forehead with magenta neat
Vibrant red of the blood that drips,
        what then is the tint of your tongue and feet?

Here now, in a moment there
        you keep appearing everywhere
I want you with me forever,
        how to bind your feet together?

And then strikes a divine thought
        With my Ida and Pingala, your feet I will tie
I will imprison you in my Sahasrar, O Ma
        and keep a watch with my third eye

Not given to be bound at one place,
        You will try to flee the grip of mine
A perennial tug of war will then begin
        between my devotion and power of thine

Who will win and who will lose?
        I know from within, I am very sure
I'll never give up and leave your feet
        With peals of laughter you will admit defeat

With You in my being—I become AUM

*A vivid portrayal by Monima of her expanded state of being
starting from an insignificant level and stretching out to the
universal and boundless principle that she calls AUM.*

Your abundance pours on me
     without being asked
Far beyond expectations
     in Your glory I bask

Whether road ahead or in the lanes gone by,
Wherever I see, only You meet my eye

You shine and glow ever in the light of mine
What I scent within is perfume of thine

Deluded people think it's me they see
Blind they are towards You besides me

It's Your fragrance alone that pervades every inch.
Sadly no one realizes and none understand the cinch

Pardon the fools, pardon the blind
Pardon the ignorant with egoistic mind

AUM was the beginning and beyond the end is AUM
With You in my being I become AUM

I am AUM, I am AUM, I am AUM

অনুভব
1987

যেমন দেখি, যেমন শিখি, যেমন করি অনুভব,
তেমন বলি, তেমন লিখি, তেমন ঠিক বিষয়ই সব।

সত্য কথায় লজ্জা, মান, ভয় করত নাই।
মিথ্যা ছাড়ি, সত্য থেকে নেব সকলেই।
শূন্য বসি, শূন্য চলি, শূন্য ঘুরি চারপাশ।
শূন্য মায়া ভেঙে আমি শরীর ছাড়ি ধরে মন।
শূন্য দিয়ে অঙ্ক করি, হৃদয় দিয়ে মিলাই প্রশ্ন।
শূন্য দিয়ে অধঃপনে ঘটিয়ে যমকি মহাবিলীন।
শূন্য দিয়ে শুরু করি, শূন্য দিয়ে করি শেষ।
শূন্য সাধন করতে করতে খুঁজে পাই না অবশেষ।

EPILOGUE

Experiencing The Nothingness

All that I see, all that I learn
And all that I feel, be with pain or pleasure
That alone I recount, only that I preach
That is truly my only treasure

Fear can't deter me, nor can shame stop me
From walking the righteous road
Unallured by the glitter of falsehood
Truthfulness remains my life-abode

I turn inwards and meditate
I experience the deep Nothingness
I look up and when I reach out
I walk into the same Nothingness

Casting away my mortal shell
My mind flies into the Void
As from zero rises the gamut of math
Every moment in time, comes from the timeless Void

Out of Nothingness do all actions emerge
Into Nothingness all reactions submerge
Before the beginning was the Nothingness
After the end remains pure Nothingness

I feel from within
My Being is that little something
Which will dissolve into the 'Great Nothing!'

This indeed is experiencing the Nothingness,
the pacific Nothingness!

GLOSSARY

Adi Shankaracharya: The foremost Hindu spiritual philosopher of the eighth century who revived and spread Adwait philosophy all over. He was considered to be an incarnation of Lord Shiva.

Adwait: Non-dualism.

Atman: The Universal Principle residing in the Self.

AUM: The timeless origin of everything.

Avatar: Incarnation.

Bhav: All pervading sentiment.

Bhavani: Goddess granting all boons.

Bhavasagar: The ocean that is life.

Brahman: Absolute, indivisible consciousness that is omnipresent in the Universe.

Dhyana: Meditation.

Gadadhar: Shri Ramkrishna Paramhansa was born Gadadhar Chattopadhyaya.

Gopal: Synonym of Lord Krishna; an avatar of Lord Vishnu.

Gopis: The playmates of Lord Krishna in Vrindavan with whom he played Raas Krida, the celestial dance.

Guru: The master who dispels the darkness of ignorance. He walks the disciple on the path to salvation. He takes charge of the disciple's life, protecting him from pitfalls.

Guru-mandal: Gurus of the same genealogy.

Hara: Synonym of Lord Shiva, the dissolver.

Ida: Ida, Pingala and Sushumna are the three main passages in a human body for life-energy transmission as per Hindu Yoga shastra.

Jai ho: A salutation pronouncing universal benediction.

Janmashtami: The day on which Lord Krishna was born.

Jogeshwari Bhairavi: An ascetic woman skilled in Tantra and Vaishnava bhakti who was the first spiritual teacher of Ramkrishna Paramhansa. She reckoned that Ramkrishna Paramhansa was an avatar.

Kailas: A snow-clad peak in the Himalayas, considered to be the abode of Lord Shiva.

Kailaspati: Lord of Kailas, i.e., Lord Shiva.

Kali: A ferocious form of the Sacred Feminine.

Kalpataru: As per Hindu mythology, this is the tree that grants all desires of the one sitting beneath it.

Kamarpukur: The birthplace of Ramkrishna Paramhansa in Bengal, India.

Kameshwar: Synonym of Lord Shiva.

Krishna: The eighth avatar of Lord Vishnu, the sustainer.

Kriya: The holy science and practice that helps one to connect to God, to get God's love flowing through you until you become one with God.

Kundalini: As per Yoga, the primordial energy lying coiled at the base of the spine, in the form of a sleeping serpent. It is envisioned as a Goddess. Its awakening results in deep meditation, enlightenment and bliss.

Leela: Divine play.

Madhusudan: Synonym of Lord Krishna.

Ma: Mother.

Mahavatar: A great spiritual Himalayan living master said to be ageless and believed to be an incarnation of Lord Shiva.

Mahesh/Maheshwar: Synonym of Lord Shiva, the dissolver.

Meera: Legendary devotee of Lord Krishna. She was an embodiment of complete surrender.

Nateshwar: Synonym of Lord Shiva, Lord of all dancers.

Pingala: See Ida.

Purush: The cosmic masculine principle.

Raas Krida: The Divine Dance that Lord Krishna performs with gopis.

Rabindranath Tagore: A nineteenth century polymath from Bengal, India. He reshaped the region's literature and music and was the first non-European Nobel Laureate (Literature). He was fondly called Gurudev.

Radha: Companion of Lord Krishna. She symbolizes immortal love.

Ramkrishna Paramhansa: A nineteenth century mystic of India born in Kamarpukur, Bengal, India. He was believed to be an incarnation of God and propounded that all religions lead to the same God.

Rudra: Synonym of Lord Shiva, the dissolver, in a ferocious form.

Sadhana: A spiritual practice consciously systematized. Its objective is purification of the Self ultimately leading to liberation.

Sahaj bhav: An all-pervading sentiment of being completely at ease.

Sahasrar: The seventh primary energy center as per yogic beliefs located at the crown of the head with a thousand petals, known as the Supreme center of contact with God.

Sakhya bhav: An all-pervading sentiment of friendship and closeness.

Samskars: The teachings during upbringing that mould a personality.

Shakti: The Sacred Feminine; the consort of Shiva. Shiva and Shakti form Complete Unity.

Shankar: A serene form of Lord Shiva, the dissolver.

Sharda Ma: Born Sharadamani Mukhopadhyaya, she was the wife and spiritual counterpart of Ramkrishna Paramhansa. She played an important role in the growth of the Ramkrishna movement, whose followers regard her as an incarnation of Divine Mother.

Shastra: Science.

Shiva: A part of the Divine Trinity (Brahma, Vishnu, Mahesh, i.e., the Creator, Sustainer and Dissolver). Shiva, also known as Mahesh, is the Dissolver.

Shravan: The month of bounty, the fifth month as per Hindu calendar.

Shriram: The seventh avatar of Lord Vishnu, the sustainer.

Swachchandanath: One of his own free will. Kashmir Shaivism describes Lord Shiva in this manner.

Tandav: The Divine Dance of Shiva.

Tara: The Sacred Feminine connoting the aspect of Universal Mother.

Thakurji: A fond epithet for Ramkrishna Paramhansa.

Umapati: Synonym of Lord Shiva, which means husband of Uma.

Vedas: Four ancient texts in Sanskrit language that contain divine knowledge revealed to seers.

Vishnu with chakra: A part of the Divine Trinity (Brahma, Vishnu, Mahesh, i.e., Creator, Sustainer, Dissolver); Vishnu is the sustainer; Sudarshan chakra is part of Lord Vishnu's divine arsenal.

Vishwaguru: Guru of the entire universe.

Yashoda: The foster mother of Lord Shrikrishna in whose affectionate care the Lord spent his childhood.

Yoga: The science of self-realization involving physical, mental and spiritual disciplines which originated in ancient India.

Yogeshwar: A synonym of Lord Krishna; Lord of all Yogis.